BENEATH THE SURFACE

TINKLE SINGH

For the dreamers, the heartbroken, and the ones who've sobbed
into their pillow

The ones who feel deeply

I hope you find strength in your scars

Contents

Contents

Preface

In a world where emotions often go unspoken, poetry provides a voice for the heart's deepest sorrows. This collection of poems is a journey through the tangled web of human emotions, exploring themes of love, heartbreak, self-esteem, volatile emotions, and the long path to healing and finding yourself

Acceptance and moving on are crucial steps in the journey of life. In these pages, you will find poems that celebrate new beginnings and the peace that comes with finding one's inner calm. The ultimate goal is not to avoid pain but to embrace the full spectrum of human experience and find peace within ourselves.

As you read this collection, I hope you find a reflection of your own heart and a companion for your own journey. May these words inspire you to feel deeply, to love fiercely, and to find beauty in the highs and lows of life.

Thank you for taking the time to dive into this collection and for allowing these words to accompany you on your path.

Acknowledgements

Writing this feels absolutely surreal. I do not have words to describe what I am feeling at this moment.

never did i think that the first book i ever publish would be a collection of poems, i always had a dream of writing romcoms, then non fiction, but this feels exactly right. romcoms are definitely on the way though.

I am so grateful for everyone who has helped me through this, be it feedback, or simply being there for me when i needed them to be.

To Yoshaa, who never stopped believing in me, in ever single area of my life. Every single time I was behind, she was there to push me forward. I'll always be grateful to have you in my life.

To Siri and Shatakshi, thank you for being there whenever I need you, it means the world to me that i can share this with you.

To Raghav, your support is a comforting presence, thank you for every single time you listened to me when I needed you to and for all the reassurance

To my parents, thank you so much.

I am immensely grateful to myself for inspiring some of the poems within these pages and for always being there with open ears and heart. I am proud of myself to be able to take this first step.

Finally, thank you to Notion Press for the support throughout this journey. Your input and help has been invaluable.

To everyone who believed in me and this collection, I am profoundly thankful. Your support has made this dream a reality.

love and longing

1. love at first sight

Did the world go still
Or was it me
Did i hear a symphony
Pious silence in the hustle
Plain focus on you
In the midst of the crowds
A thousand different tales
Unknown and tied together
Would ours be?
Was it the breeze brushing my face
Was it the swarm of people
Moving alike but in different ways
Was it your eyes on me
Was it the stories untold
Where our tales tie together
No longer unknown
Familiarity alone
And comfort and peace
Was it the call of love
Was it the promise of forever
Was it cinema
Or was it the sight of you

Is this love at first sight?

2. misdirection

Rising voices, rising storms
Rage that flows, continues
And goes
Through them, to them
I long for the luxury of peace
Of quiet, of silence
Of the moments small
If i could, i would
Soak them all
It would be my in my mind
My heart
A place for solace
My happy place
Because around me is pain, just pain
The pain of longing
For love, for affection
And yet she remains lost
No sense of direction
Or maybe she hunts for it
At the incorrect place
She doesn't have the privilege
Of looking elsewhere

No other direction
Nothing that she finds
And so she stays there
Continues her longing
For love, for affection
And i hope someday
And her soul finds solace
Not in her memories
But through her happy place
Which now exists around her
She finds the right direction

3. where hearts collide

find a light I've never known.
A spark ignites within my chest,
a timid flame of hope,
that grows with every glance,
every stolen moment shared.
Our laughter weaves through sunlit days,
a melody familiar, comforting.
In your eyes, I see my reflection,
a mirror of dreams entwined.
Love, a steady river flowing,
carving its path through time
Your presence is a gentle tide,
washing over my guarded shores.
I trace the contours of your smile,
a map leading to uncharted places.
With each step, I stumble closer
to the edge of something beautiful.
Together, we've built a haven,
a refuge from life's storms.
Through trials and triumphs,
our love stands strong, unwavering.
We cherish the journey we've traveled,

a testament to all we've become.
Two hearts, each on their own path,
finding solace in love's embrace.
One discovering, the other knowing,
yet both entwined in this journey
of wonder, of depth,
of a love that transcends time and space

4. shattered

It was us who

Built the tender home

Love,trust,comfort

The foundation of it

How did it not take one

Thought or a fleeting moment

For you

Your eyes, once clear and kind,

now cast shadows long,

a storm behind the smile

that used to feel like home

I don't see the gleam in your eyes

Anymore, i haven't since long ago

Was it me?

The warmth we once shared

now icy with betrayal,

a chill that settles deep

within the marrow of my bones

From us it goes

To you and me

To just me

Collecting the ruins of

A castle once
Built for us
There's no us anymore

5. I regret it (do you?)

I walk the line between two worlds,
each step a thread pulled tight,
a lie woven into the fabric
of love I swore to hold.
In moments of weakness,
I wandered, seeking
a fleeting spark
in unfamiliar eyes,
the thrill of forbidden flames
dancing in my shadow.
Your trust, a fragile vase,
I shattered with careless hands,
each whispered promise
a crack in the foundation
of the world we built together.
I see the hurt
etched in your eyes,
mirrors of my own guilt
reflecting back the pain
I've stitched into our story.
I didn't mean for this,
to tear apart

what we once cherished,
but here I stand,
a monument to betrayal,
a thief of our shared dreams.
Regret, a heavy cloak,
wraps tight around my shoulders,
a weight I cannot cast aside
as I watch your tears fall
like rain upon scorched earth.
I see the love
that lingers still,
a flicker in the ashes,
and wish for words
to mend the wounds
I've carved with selfish hands.
But what solace can I offer,
what balm for broken trust?
For even in apologies,
the scars remain,
a testament to my folly.
And so, I stand here,
lost in the echoes
of my own making,
praying for forgiveness
I do not deserve,
knowing that in my betrayal,
I have betrayed myself

Your trust, a fragile vase,
I shattered with careless hands,
each whispered promise
a crack in the foundation
of the world we built together.
I see the hurt
etched in your eyes,
mirrors of my own guilt
reflecting back the pain
I've stitched into our story.
I didn't mean for this,
to tear apart
what we once cherished,
but here I stand,
a monument to betrayal,
a thief of our shared dreams.
Regret, a heavy cloak,
wraps tight around my shoulders,
a weight I cannot cast aside
as I watch your tears fall
like rain upon scorched earth.
I see the love
that lingers still,
a flicker in the ashes,
and wish for words
to mend the wounds
I've carved with selfish hands.

But what solace can I offer,
what balm for broken trust?
For even in apologies,
the scars remain,
a testament to my folly.
And so, I stand here,
lost in the echoes
of my own making,
praying for forgiveness
I do not deserve,
knowing that in my betrayal,
I have betrayed myself.

6. the many faces of love

Love is a worldwide concern that surpasses cultures, period, and even class. It is the hidden fiber that binds persons together, creating friendships that shape our use deep habits. Yet, regardless of allure universality, love debris individual of ultimate mysterious and versatile experiences famous to benevolence. It exhibits in differing forms, each accompanying its own singular traits and affect our lives. From the desirous flames of sentimental love to the enduring bonds of ancestral love, common people faces of love offer united states of america glimpse into the insights of the human soul.

Love, entirely allure forms, is a tribute to the wisdom and complicatedness of the human occurrence. It is a effective feeling that shapes our identities, influences our determinations, and guides our interplays accompanying remainder of something.

From the magic of idealistic love to the lasting bonds of classification and the essential practice of egotism, each surface of love provides to the rich curtain of our lives. Understanding and dealing with common people faces of love admits us to nurture deeper networks, acknowledge the difference of human feelings, and find message and completion in our friendships.

at war and at peace

7. i want to be a phoenix

"Embrace it"
How do you
When the mirror reflects
A fractured image
A product of your mind
Not what you see
Each flaw magnified
Each imperfection true
An uncertain hue
A limit to what is true
They say "you're art"
But are you
When the canvas remains adorned
With shades of comparison
Your eyes seek approval in every glance
A labyrinth flows through you
The dance of self esteem
She fears mistake
What if she doesn't
A fragile fortress, built
With the walls of fear
As your judgements draw near

How do you
Cease it affecting you
Within the walls
Is a flicker of light
It is your seed
Of courage, of fight
Because in vulnerability lies strength
For her to breakthrough
How do you
When you're frightened
But what if you
No longer a prisoner
Of your own fortress
Of shadows, of fear
How do you feel
When you become the phoenix
And rise
Bold and clear
You find a way home
You find peace
With the intricacies of yourself
The peace within yourself flowers
And the shadows lose their powers

8. complete

I walked through shadows,
a heart shattered,
trust fractured by betrayal's hand.
In the wake of lies,
I lost myself,
a ghost in the ruins
of what we once were.
The pain was a storm,
relentless and fierce,
each memory a reminder
of love's broken promise.
But in the chaos,
I found my strength,
a flicker of hope
in the darkness.
With each tear shed,
I washed away the remnants
of what tethered me to you,
letting go of the echoes
of deceit and betrayal.
Piece by piece,
I reclaimed my soul,

rebuilding with hands
now steady and sure.
In the mirror, I see
a reflection unburdened,
eyes bright with the light
of newfound freedom.
I have journeyed through heartache
and emerged whole,
with a heart that beats
for me alone.
This is my story,
one of resilience and renewal,
a testament to the power
of letting go
and the beauty of embracing
the person I was always meant to be.

9. I hate myself

I do not recognize him
Or her
Someone stares back at me
From the mirror
My eyes notice a soul
Etched with remarks
It sits and gathers
All of the hearts'
shattered pieces
I hear it again
Lashing against me
Echoing in my mind
Each syllable carrying loath
Each word shot to kill
Each line becomes rehearsed
Until it is the truth
And i wear my flaws
Like a shroud
Each of it is magnified
All of it is true
Maybe it'll be a day of unending sun
Or the gloom of low clouds

Maybe someday i'll deserve love
Even my own

10. ashamed

Tears from the depth of despair
is it mundane, foolish or stupid
Is it awareness of the self
Or is it a weak mind
They take me moving
In the direction of their breeze
And i float in
With resistant ease
It was the hardest thing i'd ever done
Stay, when i wanted to turn away
I pretend my feet are frozen in place
Because sometime i'll have to face
That mound of disgrace
Awaiting me with bitter warm arms
To steer me away
And so i stay frozen

chaotic currents

11. corridors of memory

The bustling chambers of memory
Resurface time and again
The chaos of quotes and echoes
Of stories and tales
Of times left behind
As they remain intertwined
In the corridors of time
The ones that bring a smile
The distant laughter, the sunny days
Before we left our own ways
Sunlit afternoons and sunsets hued
Secret hideaways that we'd looked through
She misses the wind
Meeting her chimes
She explores the corridors of time
Nostalgia, a wind
That carries the gone to the going
The going will become the gone someday
Will she cherish these too
Or will she look through
The corridors of time
Nostalgia, a bittersweet companion,

a portal to the realms of what used to be,
where laughter echoes like a timeless tune
So i linger in the realms of the past
The happy and the sad
The ones that didnt last

12. the quiet within

In the stillness of my heart, I find
A quiet peace, a tranquil mind.
The storms have passed, the waves are still,
In this serenity, I find my will.
The journey of love, of loss, of pain,
Has led me here, where I remain.
A place of calm, of gentle grace,
A sanctuary, a sacred space.
No longer bound by the fears of old,
I've found the courage to be bold.
To love myself, to let light in,
To embrace the quiet within.
For in this peace, I've found my home,
A place of solace, never alone.
The quiet within, a gift of grace,
A testament to the beauty of space.

13. a tidal wave

waves at the sea
crash and crash and crash
constantly
to no end
one moment calm
the next a storm
this force takes no form
passion flares
a caged creature
consuming all in
its fiery rage
in the chaos
I lose and find
a heart untamed
a restless mind
a mine of emotions
The tides of anger, the waves of fear
The undertow pulling me near
Yet in this tempest, I am alive
Riding the waves, I learn to survive

14. flame and fury

scorching heat
wild and grand
yet here i stand
a raging inferno
a spirits fire
burning desire
of all that is loved and lost
of the heat
that resembles the frost
ignition of anger
a fiery spark
a dance of chaos
when all is dark
it consumes all
with relentless light
a great force
a mighty light
in the aftermath
of the searing fire
anew force
a rising fire
i've learned to steer

the flames of fury
are crystal clear

emotional orphan

15. dear solitude

In the attic of my heart
Resides a locked chest
A father's care
The key to which
I never possessed
In the garden of my mind
Flowers bloom
Watered and caressed
By other souls
Bu i long only for the care of one
And it happens to reside
Eternally doomed
To her, he's the moon
There but far away
Out of reach
Considered once a source of eternal light
Now she questions the plight
Of her soul, wretched
And torn
To her, he was the moon
The prize of a ordinary night
She waits and waits and waits

But his affection remains disguised
Or is it even there
yet , in her solitude
She finds strength
She is brave, she can care
For herself
She longs for something
That was never there
She carries his absence
Like invisible scars
In the tapestry of her life
She continues to weave threads of love
And in the garden of her heart
A flower grows
And her love for herself
Eternally flows

16. i could never be her

It was the rhythm with which
I would dial the digits in
The surface felt smooth and same
I felt worse and worse
The speed increased
So did my anxiety
It had been hours babe
Where were you
But in my thoughts
Now i hug myself tighter
The wool isnt warm anymore
So arent your arms
The arms i used to
Call my home
I could go anywhere
I could be anyone
I am someone
Just a bit alone
You'd say my smile was bright
Was hers brighter
Did she make you feel
Like you are floating

Like you are lighter
Like the world is a better place
That is what you told me, babe
Was i not your safe space?
Blame, rage. Sheer pain
No more dancing in the rain
Its not us anymore
Its you and me
Its you and her
I guess i could never be her
But even at my worst
I simply had the thirst
For your love
For your desire
To be the fire

17. orphan

In a house filled with shadows
words cut through me like knives
walls remain thick with whispers
of disappointment
and dicontent
They say love should be the foundation, the gentle breeze
but in this place, it's a storm, relentless and unkind.
a constant reminder that I am not enough
Their voices rise like a tide, crashing over me,
With each word, I drown a little more,
In the sea of expectations, impossible to meet,
You'll never be what we hoped for," they say,
Each syllable a stone, heavy with disdain.
Their dreams, a cloak I'm forced to wear,
Too large, too cumbersome, suffocating my own

18. navigating parental disrespect

Family dynamics are often described as the bedrock of an individual's emotional development, a cradle of love and support that shapes one's identity. However, not all familial relationships are nurturing. When a parent continuously disrespects a child, it creates an invisible yet profound scar that influences self-esteem, relationships, and the way the child navigates the world.

In literature and psychology, the term "daddy issues" is often used to describe the complex emotional turmoil experienced by individuals who have strained or unhealthy relationships with their fathers. While the term is colloquial and sometimes reductive, it points to a deeper truth about the significant impact parental disrespect can have on one's life. This essay explores the multifaceted nature of parental disrespect and its profound implications on personal growth and self-discovery.

The ramifications of parental disrespect can be profound and long-lasting. Children who grow up in environments where their worth is constantly questioned often struggle with issues of self-esteem and self-worth. They may develop a relentless inner critic, a voice that echoes their parent's disapproval and drowns out their own self-acceptance.

As a result, many individuals find themselves in a constant state of self-doubt, questioning their abilities and decisions. This internalized disrespect can lead to a fear of taking risks, as the individual constantly fears failure and criticism. The journey towards self-discovery becomes fraught with obstacles, as the individual struggles to discern their authentic self from the distorted identity imposed upon them by their parents. Despite the deep-seated impact of parental disrespect, the path to healing and self-discovery is not only possible but also profoundly transformative. The first step in this journey is acknowledging the emotional wounds and understanding that the disrespect experienced is not a reflection of the individual's worth. This acknowledgment requires courage and introspection, as it involves confronting painful truths and reevaluating the narratives one has been told.

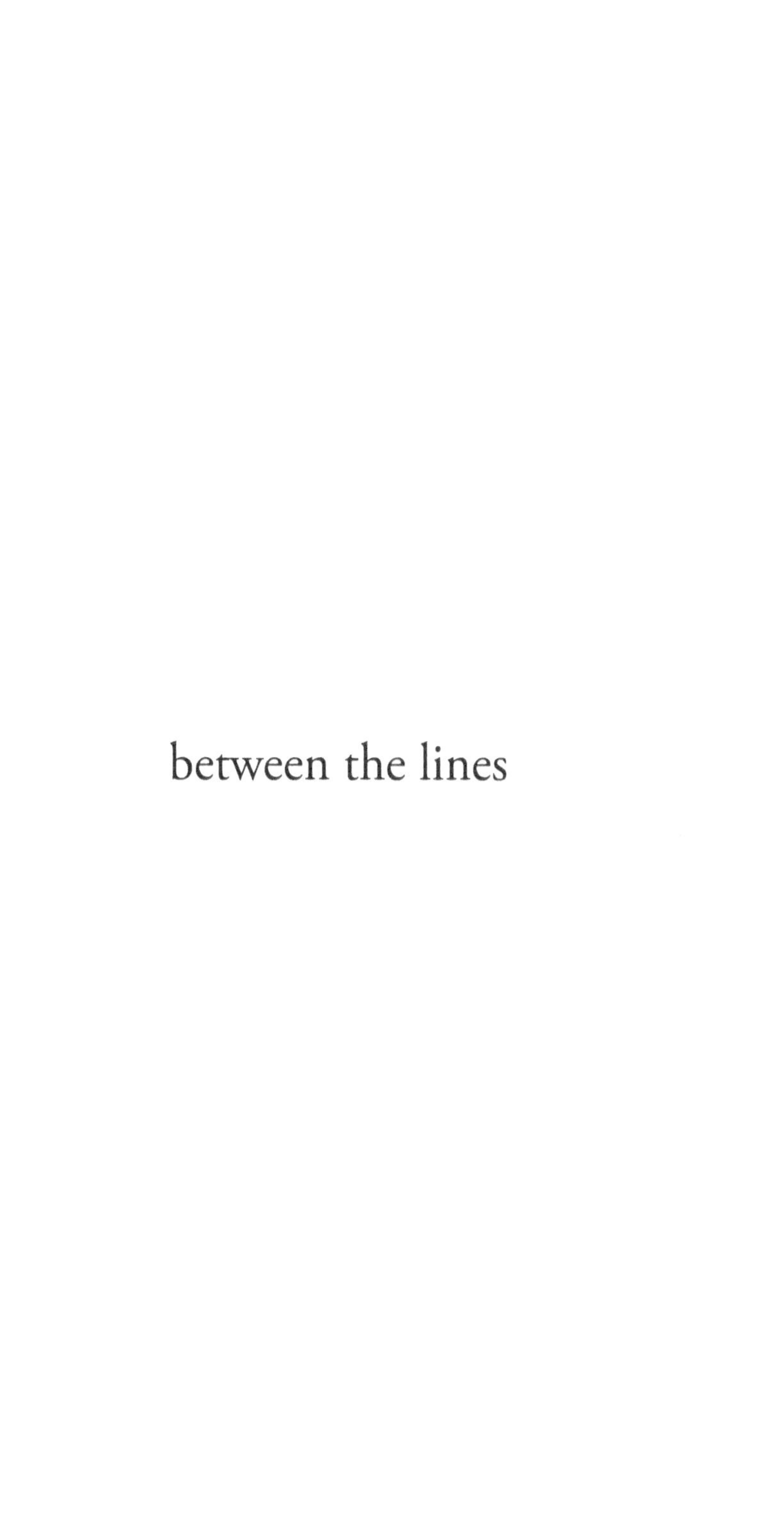

between the lines

19. the dance of seasons

Spring arrives softly,
like a whisper carried on the breeze,
a gentle hand brushing the earth awake.
The world unfurls,
petals blooming in tender hues,
promises of new beginnings scattered
like seeds across the thawing ground.
Summer bursts forth,
an exuberant celebration of life,
the sun a golden embrace wrapping around us.
Days stretch lazily,
time suspended in the shimmer of heat waves,
laughter echoing through endless evenings,
the sky a canvas painted with sunsets.
Autumn creeps in quietly,
a subtle shift in the air,
leaves relinquishing their grip,
falling in a slow, deliberate dance,
a tapestry of crimson and gold.
The world exhaling,
a sigh of acceptance
as the days shorten,

the light softens.
Winter stands still,
a hush enveloping the earth,
the world wrapped in a quilt of white.
Breath visible in the icy air,
trees etched in silver,
each branch a delicate sculpture
against the pale sky.
Silence reigns,
a reminder of the beauty
found in stillness,
a moment of pause
before the cycle begins anew.
In this dance of seasons,
we find ourselves mirrored
in nature's ebb and flow,
each moment a step in the rhythm
of life, love, and loss.
A reminder that time is a circle,
and in each ending,
a beginning waits,
ready to bloom.

20. the weight of words

In the quiet corners of a conversation,
a single word can hold the world,
tipping the balance between
love and loss,
hope and despair.
A simple utterance,
a tangled web of meaning,
a lifeline or a weapon
in the space between breaths.
We shape them with intention,
or release them carelessly,
watching as they flutter,
fall,
or soar
in the expanse of our lives.
They build bridges,
or burn them down,
construct worlds,
or tear them apart.
In the silent aftermath,
we gather their remnants,
piece together the fragments,
search for solace
in the spaces they leave behind.
For words, once spoken,
cannot be retrieved,
but linger in the heart,

an indelible mark on the soul.
So we choose them with care,
each syllable a thread,
woven into the fabric of understanding,
or a shard of glass,
cutting through the tender flesh
of human connection.
And in this dance of language,
we find ourselves reflected,
defined by the weight
of the words we hold,
the stories we tell,
the promises we keep
or break
in the quiet moments
of our shared existence.

21. capture

In love's embrace, we find our way,
Through heart's soft whispers, come what may,
Resilient souls, we rise anew,
To dance with hope, to love and bloom.

22. silence

Between the lines of what we dare to say,
Lives a world of untold hopes and dreams,
A space where our deepest fears play,
Where love's true essence silently gleams.
In the void between our spoken lines,
A secret garden blooms without a name,
Where hearts intertwine and souls align,
In this quiet realm, our passions flame.
Each unspoken word is a seed of hope,
A promise of what could yet be,
In the space where possibilities elope,
We find the courage to set our spirits free.
This realm of silence, vast and profound,
Is where our true selves come alive,
In the in-betweens, love is unbound,
In this hidden space, we thrive.
So let us cherish the words unsaid,
The pauses where our souls connect,
For in this silent dialogue, we are led,
To the beauty we often neglect.

23. spaces

In the spaces where words lose their might,
A yearning lingers, aching to be free,
A symphony of feelings, dark and bright,
Hidden behind a facade of glee.
The heart speaks volumes in a quiet sigh,
In gentle gestures, in a touch, so slight,
A spark that twinkles in an eye,
Unvoiced longings flutter and multiply.
Through every glance, every stolen touch,
Unspoken desires weave a tangled web,
Longing for connection we crave so much,
Where dreams of the heart begin to ebb.
Yet these desires are hidden deep within,
Behind layers of walls we've built so high,
A tapestry woven from where we've been,
In between lines where truth and secrets lie.
So we dance this dance of silent desire,
In shadows where fear and hope reside,
But amidst the flames of this secret fire,
Love finds a way to turn the tide.

24. the veil

In the stillness of the night, the shadows creep,
A quiet whisper in the dark, where secrets sleep.
Death stands waiting, a solemn guest,
In the gentle hush where life finds rest.
The clock ticks softly, time unwinds,
In the echo of the hour, a moment binds.
A journey taken, one last breath,
Into the arms of silent death.
The stars above in solemn gaze,
Illuminate the fleeting days,
Of life, so vibrant, now so still,
As time bends gently to its will.
In the heart of night, a candle glows,
A flickering light in the breeze that blows.
Memories dance in the shadow's embrace,
Lingering traces of a beloved face.
Death does not boast, nor does it weep,
It cradles all in its endless sleep.
A keeper of stories untold, unknown,
A voyage to realms that are never shown.
For some, it's a thief that steals the light,
A cruel end to the wondrous flight.

Yet for others, a release from pain,
A gentle peace in the falling rain.
In the silence, we ponder the unknown,
The places where our souls have flown.
Is there a dawn beyond this night,
A realm of joy, a place of light?
Death, a mystery we cannot grasp,
Its tender touch, its chilling clasp.
Yet in its shadow, we find the grace,
To cherish each day, each fleeting trace.
The seasons turn, the earth renews,
A cycle of life, a perpetual muse.
Death, the curtain that softly falls,
As life dances on, as the echo calls.
For in the end, we are all the same,
Returning to the earth from whence we came.
In death, a part of us lingers on,
A whisper in the wind, a song at dawn.
In the heart of night, where shadows play,
Death waits patiently to lead the way.
But fear not, for in its gentle hand,
Lies the promise of a distant land.

25. unpredictable

Life moves without asking permission,
a river flowing, cutting through stone,
carving new paths where dreams dare to wander.
It is a whispering wind, unseen and unexpected,
blowing through the fields of our existence,
lifting the leaves of our plans,
scattering them like whispers
into the vast unknown.
Days tumble like dice, a roll of fate,
each number a possibility, a surprise,
crafted from moments we never imagined,
painted in colors we've never seen.
The sun rises with a palette of promises,
only to set with a symphony of surprises,
a reminder that life is
the art of embracing the unforeseen.
We make plans, chart courses, draw maps
on the fragile parchment of our desires,
only to have them torn and rewritten
by the hands of time,
by the chaos that dances,
invisible threads weaving through the tapestry,

intertwining joy and sorrow,
strength and fragility,
a dance of paradox,
a ballet of contradictions.
In the echoes of laughter and tears,
we find the rhythm of resilience,
the courage to step onto the stage
of uncertainty,
to dance with the shadows and the light,
to let go of the fear of the unknown,
to leap into the air, trusting
that the ground will catch us.
For life is not a line, straight and narrow,
but a winding road of twists and turns,
where every corner hides a secret,
every bend a mystery waiting to unfold,
and we, the explorers of this realm,
venture forth with hearts open wide,
seeking the beauty hidden in chaos,
the wisdom wrapped in the unpredictable.
In the silence between breaths,
we hear the stories of stars,
ancient and eternal,
telling tales of galaxies born from chaos,
of order emerging from disorder,
a universe that expands and contracts,
like the heartbeat of existence,

a reminder that change is the only constant,
that life is a poem written in free verse,
lines that flow without structure,
without rhyme,
but with a rhythm all their own.
And so, we embrace the dance of uncertainty,
the unpredictable song of life,
with arms wide open,
with eyes that see beyond the horizon,
knowing that the journey is the destination,
and every step we take
is a part of the story we create.
For in this dance, we find our truth,
in the chaos, we find our strength,
and in the unpredictability of life,
we discover who we are,
we find the beauty
in being beautifully unsure.

Author's Note

Writing this collection has been a profound journey of self discovery, and a rollercoaster of emotions that i've experienced. Each poem within these pages is a glimpse into the complexities of love, identity, and the scars left by those who shape us. It is a testament to the resilience of the human spirit and our capacity to heal and grow despite the challenges we face.

The inspiration for this collection came from a lot of personal experiences, but also a fictional character I created in my head. Acknowledging this also means that I am scared to admit that i might have not done a lot of these emotions and experiences the justice they deserved. However, I am proud of creating a space and giving myself a chance to explore these emotions within the pages of this book.

I hope these poems resonate with you and provide solace, inspiration, or simply a moment of reflection. My wish is for this book to be a companion on your journey, reminding you of the strength and beauty that lies within, even amidst the chaos.

Thank you for allowing me to share this collection with you.

With gratitude,

Tinkle